SILHOUETTES

AT DUSK

I ripped out
two pages,
don't tell
anyone. :)

Writer's
Pocket

First published by Writer's Pocket in 2021

email: publish@writerspocket.com

Copyright © 2021 Writer's Pocket

edited by Garima Vyas

cover design by Bimal Kirti

All rights reserved.

ISBN: 1956528022

ISBN-13: 9781956528022

www.writerspocket.com

CONTENTS

1. Would You Weep If I Died?
Jolina McConville

Bio: I'm an Asian-American writer and have been writing for several years - mostly prose, but in the past few years, I've had an interest in writing poems. Reading and writing are a passion of mine, as well as music - I'm a violinist. I spend much of my free time reading, writing, and listening to and playing music. I can write in many different genres but I enjoy things inspired by my own experiences.

Email: jaymaymac@yahoo.com

*****

Would you weep if I died?
If the breath were stolen from my lungs,
If the timpani in my breast were to cease playing,
And my limbs go limp?

Would you weep if I died?
My hands cold as stone,
And my lips and cheeks pale,
And eyes fluttered shut and voice silent forevermore?

Would you weep if I died,
And simply stopped living?
Would your heart twist in your chest and sorrow crush you,
Or would you move on?

Would you weep if I died,
Or find another?
Would my death make an impact,
Or be merely a ripple in a lake?

Would you weep if I died,
If you were no longer to feel my touch,
Or kiss my mouth,
Or entwine your fingers in mine?

Would you weep if I died,
If our future were stolen?
Would it be a tragic love story,
Like Romeo and Juliet is considered to be?

Would you weep if I died?
Would the grief be overbearing?
Would you be unable to eat or sleep,
Knowing I would never again stand by your side?

Would you weep if I died?
Would I be easily forgotten,
The remnants of an old love,
As you move to a new one?

Would you weep if I died,
Or would you express short grief and leave?
Do I mean enough that it would shatter you,
And tear you to bits?

Would you weep if I died,

The way I would you?
Would it feel like the ground opened under you,
Your world crashing down around you?

Would you weep if I died,
Loud cries in the day,
Silent sobs in the night,
Hands over your mouth to stifle your voice?

Would you weep if I died
And make the pain worse,
By remembering every moment,
Every touch, every word?

Would you weep if I died?
Would hot tears stream down your cheeks?
Would your eyes be red and puffy,
As your shoulders shake?

Would you weep if I died?
Would you feel an empty hole?
Would it feel like a huge loss?
Would my absence be crippling?

Would you weep if I died?
If my laugh were never to ring,
Or my smile to shine,
Or my eyes to twinkle?

Would you weep if I died?
A silly question, I know.
But still, my heart aches with it -

Would you weep if I died?

2. The Pebble
Jolina McConville

Bio: I'm an Asian-American writer and have been writing for several years - mostly prose, but in the past few years, I've had an interest in writing poems. Reading and writing are a passion of mine, as well as music - I'm a violinist. I spend much of my free time reading, writing, and listening to and playing music. I can write in many different genres but I enjoy things inspired by my own experiences.

Email: jaymaymac@yahoo.com

*****

A damaged pebble erst admired,
Told the whisperings of accepting tenderness
Until once no longer desired,
Tossed aside as if effortless.

Cast out it sunk into the river,
Lost in the darkness, deprived of a home,
The light shining - hardly a sliver,
Doomed to sit forever alone.

Until by chance it was picked up by a seeker.
Once treated as a throwaway,
Now embraced and no longer the weaker,
Here to stay.

But now as a treasure,
Blessed with love that has no measure.

3. We Are All Broken Souls
Rutuja Manoj Rane

Bio: Data scientist by profession and poet by passion, I am a 24-year-old New Yorker working in the financial industry, observing things, people and places as I explore life. There is poetry in everything around us, and that's my inspiration. I write about nature, life, emotions and human reactions - for what are we without the world, and what is the world without us!

Instagram: blink_of_ink

*****

We are all broken souls:
Dangling dandelions against the strength of the storms,
Storms that rage inside our hearts,
Storms that rival the typhoons outside,
That run us out of breath
Having taken our breath away at first,
That turn into a sleepless nightmare
Having started as a daisy daydream at first.

We are all wandering souls:
Deaf daffodils against the blaring sounds of our hearts,
Hearts that break and burn,
Hearts that fall and twist and turn,
That have tried one too many chairs
Having loved each one as if it were the last,
That store memories that tear a void inside

7

Having filled it with love and joy it thought would last.

We are all wreaked souls:
Dreary daisies weakened in the tide that washes away
the shore,
Dull dawns and eerie evenings coupled with broken
bones,
Smiling away in the heat of the day to soak our pillows
with salty tears in the night.

We are all soft souls:
Searching for love,
Reaching for care,
Yearning for touch,
All keeping our hearts bare.

We are all brave souls:
Holding our hearts on our sleeves,
Giving all there is to give,
In the only hope - that one day one shall receive -
A love to love for all of the time,
A precious on whom to spend the dime,
A someone who'd make simple things in life sublime,
A verselet to complete this verse of mine in rhyme.

4. The Misfits
Rutuja Manoj Rane

Bio: Data scientist by profession and poet by passion, I am a 24-year-old New Yorker working in the financial industry, observing things, people and places as I explore life. There is poetry in everything around us, and that's my inspiration. I write about nature, life, emotions and human reactions - for what are we without the world, and what is the world without us!

Instagram: blink_of_ink

*****

The rising moon to the sun setting in the west,
The shining stars to the moon smiling at his best,
Ocean waves to the sands in the desert,
The unkindled flame to the darkness that manifests.

The torch of truth to the lies untold,
The touch of joy to the mourning household,
Purple skies to the afternoon heat bold,
The metamorphosis of a cactus into a marigold.

5. I Don't Like You
Jadyn

Bio: I'm just a 16 year old trying to make something of herself :)

*****

i don't like you,
i don't like you yet you're the one i look for in every crowded room,
the one i catch myself fixing myself for,
the one that i wish would see me on my good days.
i don't like you but you're the one i want to talk to every day
and i want you to want to talk to me.
i wish i could build that connection with you that i am so longing for,
the one that i've never had with anyone before,
the one that brings me comfort just thinking about it.

i don't like you but i still get jealous when you talk to others and not me,
when you post about someone else when i've never been posted about,
when you take too long to reply
and i start wondering if you're talking to someone better.
i'm jealous,
i'm jealous of all of the girls that get your attention
and all of the guys that get to be your friends,
i'm jealous of all of the people that have built a bond

with you
because i want that too,
and when i'm jealous it starts to make me wonder,
do i like you?
more importantly, do you like me?

no, it can't be
you don't talk to me enough to like me,
you don't try to spend every moment with me like i so
wish you would,
you don't worry about who i'm talking to or what i'm
doing,
you couldn't like me,
not a chance.

but then there are those moments,
those moments when your eyes linger
just a little longer than everyone else's when i walk into
the room,
those moments that i catch you staring
whenever i'm doing just some little things,
when i'm laughing with someone else
and see you watching out of the corner of my eye.
those moments make me think i might have a chance,
that i might be able to connect with you on such a level
that we know each other's thoughts,
such a level that we're breathing the same air constantly
because it's all we know,
but am i right?
is it real?
do we have something more than a nonexistent
friendship?

are we more than just acquaintances?
either way,
i suppose it does not matter

why, you ask?
because i don't like you.

6. Guilty
Joaraliz T Jimenez

Bio: I'm a 25-year-old psychology student who has made writing her escape. I find inspiration in not only my experiences but in other people's as well. I am obsessed with becoming better each day and I imbibe a lot of softness and heartfelt expression in my poetry. I hope to inspire others with my originality today and always.

Instagram: joaraliztalishax

*****

You feel safe, don't you?
(Caresses my face with his cheek)
Wanna look away, don't you?
Your heart struggles to breathe
And your stomach sinks,
When you can't find your sleep
Those thoughts in your head
Are hard to release.

Those butterflies you feel,
They're new to you,
Those dreams you keep having
Got used to you.
Pushing away what you love,
Not knowing right from wrong,
The fingertips I massaged
Weren't mine for long.

One million thoughts of you, 24/7
And not one without you.
I see myself with you and you with me.
Love hits different when there's a safe place to speak
The world looks different when I'm the only one you see
The truth tastes different when there's room to breathe.
Love, that's love, those nerves in your hands,
They can't stop shaking so they expand.
Here your heart will properly heal
I'm your medicine, I'll heal your spills,
So tell me that you'll put your heart in it.
I love you and you love me despite the flaws in this.
Let me stay in your world, don't let me come out of it
I'm ready to fall in love by accident.

7. Goodbye
Landon Halladay

Bio: I love music, and writing just comes to me naturally. As a way to write a story and express my self on the paper.

Email: landonhalladay@gmail.com

*****

The most painful word I've ever heard:
"Goodbye"

The word that tore my heart to pieces.

The word that took something so pure and fragile,
a memory worth a thousand lifetimes,
torn to shreds in mere moments.

Untainted love, slipping through my fingers like sand.

Gone.

Fading from existence but not from my memories.

No matter how hard I try.

8. I Knew This Girl
Alexya

Bio: I use poetry to let every emotion I have spill. It's like a therapy session for me. I can always count on my poems to make me feel better.

Instagram: alexya_garcia12

*****

I knew this girl
Who always imagined,
What was love like?

Was it sweet
With butterflies
And a happily ever after?

Was it true love at first sight
And you knew then and there
That you'll be together for infinity?

I knew this girl
Who tried dating
And tried to figure out what love was like.

At first, it was sweet
With butterflies, and she thought
Maybe it was happily ever after,
But then they broke her.

She was left a mess
But still wanted the love
She had longed for.

I knew this girl
Who tried to hide the hurt
And tried to date again.

She locked eyes with a boy,
She forgot the pain she felt in the past
And went all in and loved this boy

She was thinking that it might
Be true love at first sight,
She wanted to be with him till eternity.
Sadly, he hurt her too.

I knew this girl who
Wanted to know,
What was love like?

Now she wished she never knew.

9. Morning Rises
Yahir Ronquillo-Ojeda

Bio: I love to read and write, and I'm a musician by profession.

Instagram: toasty_juice_box27

*****

If the sun has the strength to rise, why can't I?
If the sun didn't rise tomorrow,
Everyone would care
But if I didn't rise tomorrow,
All I would get is a bunch of weird stares
For I am not the sun,
But neither are you.
But the difference between you and me
Is that I would've checked to see
If you were okay that next morning
And the fact that you're with me makes me happy.
And I smile every day for the fact that you take away
half of my pain
But I still have half of that pain
And it hurts and it kills me to say
That I don't think I'll ever be partially okay.
I don't think I'll ever be more than enough,
More than just another tool covered in rust,
The one that no one cares to use just because it isn't
brand new

But let me tell you something I do the same shit that you
do,
All I need is someone's help to get me unoxidized,
For this pain that I have is nowhere near faded
But all I need is someone to help me,
Someone to care they could be a pretty girl,
With pretty eyes and pretty long hair.
But if I'm being honest I don't really care,
I just need someone to help,
Can you please help me?

10. Because of You
Hailey Culbertson

Bio: I'm 16 and I love Taylor Swift.

Instagram: haileyculbertson_

*****

the rose bush in my garden was once beautiful,
red roses, white roses, pink roses,
it was not shielded with a fence,
they were a beauty that should be shared with the world.

then you came and stole all the roses,
now there is no beauty to be shared with the world.
the only thing left in my garden is the thorns,
you're the one who stole the beauty from the garden,
yet you blame me when your finger gets pricked.

now i work to rebuild the roses
but every time i blossom a new one, you still come and
steal it,
tossing vilification as you do.
i have no choice but to build a fence to keep you out
but now everyone else is kept out too.

11. 2020
Jelaila Harris

Bio: I am a very emotional being so when something triggers me I am already making up poems in my head. I am a junior, a Sagittarius and I love adventures.

Instagram: onchilllaii

*****

Deprived of sleep,
As our feet continuously beat,
No rest,
No justice,
No peace.

Shipwrecked at heart,
Iron feet,
Our mind is enslaved,
Our body is like a sculpture,
Wanting to move but we can't.

Our hearts are bleeding and I do not mean the way it's supposed to,
We are enslaved in our thoughts,
Our mind
And
Even our soul.

Tired,

How about fatigue,
Hesitating to speak because you might be next in line for
a story,
It's easier to get rid of the problem than solve it,
Right?

We just want to breathe,
Be free from our demons,
We want to run,
Jump
And scream.

Anything to have us feeling alive,
We just want to come home.

Heartbreak,
How about misery,
Mourning the death of ourselves,
Killing off the last of our language so we can just fit in,
We have never been normal
And that's
Okay.

Trying,
I see you trying to be the best you can
But
Also let yourself breathe,
Let yourself fall,
Sink,
Disconnect.
You've been on autopilot,
You're exhausted,

Pain is the epitome of beauty,
It's always something you can take away from the dark,
The dark is needed.

Healing will not always be a beautiful catastrophe
But in the end you will see what He has planned for you.

I congratulate those who have found themselves,
Those who didn't know where to go or where home even
was
But continued to search,
Those who have lost everything but still they stood on
all 10,
Those with mental health issues,
Those who were on the line of giving up
And also those who have been abused.

I stand with you,
We stand with you,
You are not alone!

As we look back on 2020,
The year of transformation,
The year of revolution,
The year of perseverance
And the year of change.

There is suffering behind those working hands
And pain behind those forced hard truths,
I'm sorry but not sorry to say that my people are the
backbone of this country.

We are more than conquerors.

12. Peaches
Madelaine

Bio: I am a high school student and enjoy playing with my dogs and reading.

Instagram: maddy.under.hill

*****

Peaches rot on the nearby trees
That gather, judgemental, in a row,
A web of tangled, mangled thoughts
Spreads from the trees, roots
Killing anything good that might have once lived
In the pleasant mind, alongside the peaches.

Envy struck the peaches,
It rotted them right off the trees.
Once upon a time they lived,
Thoughts neatly organized in a row
And now they are messy, a tangle of roots
Until all that's left are the unpleasant thoughts.

They crept in, those sneaky little thoughts
That festered until they overshadowed the peaches.
Without sunlight, they died, the plant rotted down to the roots,
I'm stuck inside these dead trees
With only memories of the tidy, neat row,
The place in my mind where the peaches once lived.

It was where a happier version of myself lived
Void of any intrusive, angry, sad thoughts.
I could go anywhere, across the ocean I would row
But now I am stuck with the smell of these rotting
peaches.
My sunlight is deprived by the dark branches of the trees
And what is still growing is twisted, angry roots.

They let out a yelp, those nasty roots,
They startle anyone still alive, leaving only those who
have lived.
All that's left are the people that have the same dark,
rotting trees,
It's not important anymore, we have the same thoughts.
Poisoned by the same time and ageing, your rotting
apples fall beside my peaches,
The rotten fruit falls in organized rows.

They sink into the soil, in the same neat rows,
They grow their own roots,
Stunted with the lack of sun, trees of apples and peaches,
Despite the circumstances, they lived.
From death, emerges life and from life new thoughts,
A new me, new us, new trees.
We grow in perfect rows and grow over the trees that
once lived,
We create new roots for ourselves, we create new
thoughts
We grow new peaches, we become new trees.

13. Matches
Madelaine

Bio: I am a high school student and enjoy playing with my dogs and reading.

Instagram: maddy.under.hill

*****

It is dark in this room,
The thoughts creep in,
Scratching at the walls of this tomb,
They always win.

The paint is chipped in here,
The walls, crumbling and old.
Seeping in from the cracks is fear,
Wet, harsh, and cold.

I try to swim to the top,
Gasping for air,
My lungs feel as though they'll pop,
I let go of every care.

I embrace the dark.
In the distance, matches spark.

14. I Remember
Ivan Acevedo

Bio: I can usually be found reading a book, and that book can encompass multiple genres. When not engrossed by literary wonders, I love creative writing, engage in photography, immerse myself in philosophy, and otherwise spend far too much time reading up on random topics. I live in Los Angeles, with my family and my lovable menagerie of cats.

Email: aceveiva003@gmail.com

*****

I remember your hair,
Cascading down in waves of fire
Like an ocean of burning embers
That my hands may sail through
In the gentlest of nights.

I remember your eyes,
A place where you kept the stars,
Silver-blues trapped in the embrace of sapphire halos
As if they wielded both the moon and seas.
Flecks of vivid darks dashed across fields of earthbound skies,
Sinking and drowning into gateways to your soul held in their centres,
A place where I too drowned.

I remember your skin,
Incarnate of moonlight,
Gentle and soft
Like silken drapes,
Beauty kept in such fragility,
The vessel that bore your soul,
Something I adored,
Something I felt burning in mine.

I remember your face,
Sculpted by the gods themselves,
Something you loathed,
Something I loved.
I had never grown to adore the stars so much
Until I had seen
The constellations painted across your cheeks
And the bridge of your nose.

I remember your touch
After you left it lingering softly on my cheeks
Or besides me in the dead of night,
Something I still feel
Like phantom pains
So real though just out of reach.

I remember your voice
Like that of an angel's,
It brought a sense of peace
Like morning birdsong.
Never rough,
Silent and subtle,
Carrying warmth and love with it.

Eloquence and beauty,
Mellifluous, like a harmonious melody,
Singing softly unto the heavens,
Something I still hear echoing back from nowhere.

I remember your love,
Something I can only describe
As the humbling mountains,
The sighing trees,
The whispering sands,
The singing seas,
The weeping rain,
The fervent sun
And the mourning moon.
Like a flame in my heart,
Holding it so closely
To protect me in the bitterness of winter.

Forever and always,
I remember you.

15. Of The Things She Creates
Laci Powell

Bio: If there's one thing a lot of people know about me, it's that I have a passion for writing. I hope one day to become a published fiction author and have a way of seeing beauty and peace in the chaos.

Email: lpowell5655@gmail.com

*****

I thank the earth for her magic and materials,
For soft damp soil and warm dry sand.
For gorgeous stone formations, crystals and stalagmites.
Wildflower fields, rugged mountains, oceans cavernous.
Her skin nurtures and is nurtured of greens, blues, and
yellows.
And her callused hands shape our very existence.

Every event leads back to her,
phenomenons,
disasters,
miracles.
All that is here, from fossils to clouds.
Loud, silent,
Large, dainty,
Complicated, simple.
She creates and restricts,
Beauty both within her bones and atop her flesh.

16. That One Night in January
Laci Powell

Bio: If there's one thing a lot of people know about me, it's that I have a passion for writing. I hope one day to become a published fiction author and have a way of seeing beauty and peace in the chaos.

Email: lpowell5655@gmail.com

*****

The black cat stares,
eyes glassy and of lemon hue, glowing
through the glass
and into the dull outside,
where tiny clusters of white
flutter down.
The sky seems to darken
with each passing minute,
unnerving and silent.
Leaving a pit,
gaping,
in the depths
of my chest.

My tea would cool faster
and the light would surely fade,
leaving me longing.
Once again,
I wait for another day.

17. Summer Night Crisis
Matthew

Bio: I call my Kantshens (Conscience) De' soul poet. I love to write about poems that connect to us on a deeper level, while also inspiring others through the soul. I have been writing for 8 years and I want to finally share some of my work to the world. Poetry for the soul is my goal as a poet.

Instagram: kantshens_

*****

We shed screams,
to endless echoes of defeat.

We pound the pumps of love to our pain receptors,
to only bathe in the lies designed to fry.

Demanding core peace detonates the misconception of this reality,
making it beautiful to soak in local ambitions.

You cry joy to my anger,
while blinding the sun reactor of unity,
destroying the only truth to teamwork.

This could be a summer night crisis, or
a summer day blue.

What do you choose?
Because honestly,

I just want to enjoy this summer,
without feeling like I'm going to lose.

Just for this summer.

18. What Comes out of my Mouth
Atticus Knightwood

Bio: I'm 15 years old, soon to be 16. I'm pansexual and hope to one day be an amazing author.

Email: AtticusKnightwood@gmail.com

*****

I choose to be quiet
because I hate the noise that comes out
more than ever.
The very sound of it departing from me
brings me to tears.

19. Unfinished Business
Bermina M Chery

Bio: I exist to encourage, empower, and serve the needs of others in all that I do. To do so, I consistently use my voice and actions to amplify the voices of those who are most vulnerable, overlooked, neglected, marginalized, or have been silenced within our present-day society.

Instagram: luv_life_peeps

*****

"To be, or not to be, that is the question."
What does that even mean though?
To be or not to be… what?
For me, it's to be alive or not to be alive?
Is it worth circumnavigating a world that preys on my downfall
and was never built for me to succeed?
I didn't choose this life, it chose me,
therefore, do I even want it?
However, I don't get to choose the answer to that question
because the system has already mapped out
the projection and trajectory of my life for me.
Strictly determining my success unless by redress I possess
the power to finesse the system by being
an outlier, an anomaly, an inexplicable ball of energy
that surpasses worldly comprehension

and doesn't fit the mold.

"For who would bear the whips and scorns of time, the
oppressor's wrong."
To be Black or not to be Black in a White world?
Do I love my complexion enough to endure the bigotry
and discrimination?
The misconceptions and misperceptions?
The missed opportunities, misinterpretations, and
disqualifications?
Is it really worth it when I have the capacity to just end it
all?
That's the one and only definitive choice I have,
I can choose not to be and take it all away.
So why don't I?
Why haven't I?
Most importantly, what's stopping me?
Can it be that I am afraid?
I used to be but how do you fear something you spend
every waking moment waiting for?
I don't fear death because I expect it.
I've grown accustomed to death.
Considering its deep roots within my psyche,
that comes as no surprise to me.
It desensitizes, debilitates, and destabilizes the fear
that once occupied my thoughts
by instead making a home for itself.
My expectation is that one of these days will be my last
but I simply can't pinpoint which one.
Every day, I wake up alive is a miracle
because I know that the system has pilfered the lives,
looted the souls,

and discarded the bodies of my fellow kinsmen.

"Let be."
So why do I choose to be?
I live for others, not myself.
I find my source of being through the livelihood and empowerment
of others.
This is why I know it's my purpose
to fight for the preservation and expansion of that livelihood
because I am nothing without it.
It's innate and intrinsic to my very being
which is why my indignation will rule this nation.
My dissent descends from being a descendant of activists,
carrying their unfinished business,
and pushing it closer towards the finish line.
If and when I die, it will be in the name, progression, and advancement
of the people.

If not, then I have never lived.

20. The Queen
Madeline Grajeda

Bio: I'm 17, I have a lot of pets, and I'm chronically ill.

Instagram: maddie_grajeda

*****

The queen arises with grace and beauty,
Ever so elegantly waves to the community
But hidden within her great big dwelling,
The secret that lies is quite compelling.

For when her portals close at night,
The demons in her mind come out and seek fright,
They feed on the darkness that lies in her heart
Due to the solitude that tears her apart.

But then in the break of day,
All her demons soon decay.
She puts on her mask and puts on her face
For she must hideaway her feelings and act like
everything's in place.

21. Borderline Personality Disorder
Madeline Grajeda

Bio: I'm 17, I have a lot of pets, and I'm chronically ill.

Instagram: maddie_grajeda

*****

It's hard living with borderline personality disorder,
Having unstable moods and bad relationships,
Constantly causing others pain
Due to my mind's disintegrating apocalypse.

I'm sorry for my intense mood swings,
Making me hypersensitive to others words,
One minute filled with content and the next, I'm
An evil swarm of rabid birds.

I often get impulsive thoughts
That I just can't seem to shut down,
Zoning out for hours at a time,
Causing me to have emotional breakdowns.

My relationships constantly strained
From loving someone to intense hate,
Fearing abandonment and rejection
Because my emotions always tend to dominate.

People say I'm hard to deal with
That I'm attention-seeking and self-absorbed,

But they just don't understand
That my mind is more than I can afford.

Borderline personality disorder
Is like living on a constant roller coaster,
Never knowing what's ahead
But realizing it's never over.

22. Blind Bird
Marcos Estrada

Bio: I am a poet from California and I have been writing since I was 11. All my poems derive from pain.

Instagram: meta4ic_life

*****

Have you ever seen a blind bird fly?
He just flew and flew so he wouldn't die,
his mother never knew that he couldn't see
and the bird never faced reality.
All he was worried about
was the worm his mother brought.
He said his sight would come with feathers
or so he thought
but then that moment came,
it was a dark and gloomy day
and the bird's feathers began to grow,
he was ready for the flight below
or even above, he couldn't tell.
The only thing he could do was hear or smell
but he was determined to spread his wings,
so he thought of beautiful things
like flowers and girl birds and worms
and other things but mostly worms
and there he stood,
at the edge of a branch, ready.
He spread his wings and ran,

keeping it all steady
and with one quick flap,
he flew for a second then SPLAT!
The poor bird hit the floor.
He tried again, ready to fly some more
but with every try, he would just fail.
Then one day he sat alone on a sail
thinking about how to fly without sight
then he said, "Maybe I might,"
and he took off once again.
Two seconds in he hit the floor again,
this time it was next to my feet.
I felt pity for the birds defeat
so I picked him up
and put him in a cup.
You see, I was sitting alone
in a park bench
abandoned by the woman I loved
writing poems about her,
then I skipped to the next page
of my notebook because the pain
was unbearable, so I started
writing about a blind bird
but I never knew his fate.
Now he's in a cup in my hand.
How could this be?
Is this reality?
Could this blind bird be me,
blinded by a woman's beauty?
I nursed the bird back to health
then took a nap.
When I awoke, the bird was gone

and I couldn't see;
I just sat alone in the nest,
high above the oak tree.

23. Women
Jadyn Cohee

Bio: I'm a competitive dancer, I've been dancing since I was 9 years old and I love hip hop. I've also been writing since I was 9 years old and I can write in any genre or style.

Email: Jadyncohee@icloud.com

*****

Ugh women,
So sensitive,
So dramatic,
Not submissive enough.
Always say no when I'm tryna hit,
Always think that they can dress how they want,
Always think they have the power when it's men that
run things,
Too opinionated,
Fine, you're ugly anyway,
They always have something to say.

Ugh women,
So beautiful,
So poised,
So independent,
So strong,
There's a reason the Amazons were women
Because even the Greek Gods knew

That you can never create a warrior quite like us.
Every bone in our bodies is founded in power and
strength,
Our minds are oceans that keep the world flowing,
Our hearts are pure gold with a harmony of peace and
kindness,
We are the past, present, and future
But you don't want to acknowledge that.
You want to hide us,
Belittle us,
Embarrass us,
Shame us,
Well you can strip my vocal cords from my body
And my voice will still read louder than your ignorance.
My beauty will still shine,
My spirits will still fly,
My hope will still ring to the mountaintops,
My mind will still create
But ya know, women.

24. On a Cloudy Day
Jadyn Cohee

Bio: I wrote this poem when I felt anxious, depressed and alone. My school counsellor suggested I write down the reasons that life is beautiful and what I look forward to and from there I created this poem.

Email: Jadyncohee@icloud.com

*****

Some days my world turns dark and my skies are not blue
But then again there's so much I can do,
I love the sound of old typewriters,
I love Christmas lights and fireflies; anything that makes the world glow brighter,
I love making people laugh and cracking goofy jokes.
I'm obsessed with books and all that they hold,
I enjoy sunflowers and roses and pastel colors,
I admire the trees and the breeze oh how they flow in the summer,
I love music and dancing with the unique feeling it brings,
No pun intended but these are some of my favorite things.
I look forward to the day I graduate,
I look forward to love and a bunch of fun dates,
I look forward to having great friends who love me dearly,

I look forward to the day I see the world clearly,
So when life goes wrong
And I feel alone,
I come back to these thoughts
In a place I call home.

25. Heaven's Babe
Keziah Perozzo

Bio: I'm 17 years old and I had to write a bunch of poems for school this year. At the beginning, I thought I would hate it, but it turned out to be my favorite subject. My creativity is usually best when it's past midnight.

Instagram: keziah_._._

*****

Gone tomorrow,
Hardly known.
Gone today,
Hardly grown.
Gone past,
Oh too soon.
Gone future,
A slight cycle of the moon.
          Gone
We miss you every day,
We're thankful for the way,
The way you touched our lives,
The way you stole our hearts,
The way you held such joy
From the very start,
The start that left too quick,
The start whose end made me sick.
I know you're having fun up there with all the babes,
I wish I could hold you and let you live your days

But here you'd suffer
And up there, you shine.
Earth isn't good enough to you,
Sweet baby of mine!

26. My Love
Keziah Perozzo

Bio: I'm 17 years old and I had to write a bunch of poems for school this year. At the beginning, I thought I would hate it, but it turned out to be my favorite subject. My creativity is usually best when it's past midnight.

Instagram: keziah_._._

*****

My darling, don't you know how you shine?
No, the devil seeps into my mind.
My dear, you are such a great wonder!
In my head, there's constant thunder.
My precious, your smile lights up a room.
My teeth are too yellow, it brings great gloom.
My angel, don't you know how high you can soar?
I have no confidence, I'll fall to the floor.
Sweet one, you have a heart of gold.
That doesn't matter, I think you are too cold.
My angel, fix your crown, your halo's sleeping.
It's already broken, it doesn't need fixing.
My precious, your eyes are a delight.
Okay, but my heavy eye bags will stir up a freight.
My dear, moms adore you and kids just as well.
Yeah, but teenagers scare me, it's a living hell.
My darling, stop that! You are so amazing!
Thank you, I guess I'll try to start believing.
My darling, my dear, my angel, my love,

sweet one, you are a gift from above!

27. Never Forget
Lee

Bio: I'm queer and non-binary. I have two cats and a ball python that I adore. I love chocolate and macaroni & cheese but not at the same time.

Email: rainbow.zebra.713@gmail.com

*****

There are some things
I can never forget.
The shape of her smile,
The light in her eyes.
How she doesn't know,
How I'll never tell.
And I'll never forget
The shine of a blade
Dancing over my skin.
The way fabric scratches over
My mistakes from last night.
I'll never forget
The sick relief I always feel
With the first line,
Fifth line,
Fortieth line.
How red starts to paint my legs,
And how
Good
It feels,

To not have to think,
To be free of the thoughts,
To feel alive again,
For one
(Just one)
Moment.
These I can never forget;
Though sometimes I wish I could.

28. Phoenix Girl
India-Mae Fraser

Bio: I am a 16-year-old writer. I love theatre, reading, writing and dancing. I'm the youngest of three girls and I hope to eventually be an English and theatre teacher as well as publish some books.

Instagram: stars_and_the_moon_and_me

*****

Imagine:
The queer teen cuts her hair short for the first time
And suddenly a whole world of possibilities opens up to her,
Like she's being born anew,
She suddenly knows where she's going.

Imagine:
The queer teen dyes her hair bright orange for the first time
And suddenly a whole world of fire opens up to her
Like she's the phoenix from the flames,
Nobody knows just how high she aims.

Imagine:
She shoots for the moon because even if she misses, she'll land among stars,
She faces a history and future free from scars,
She bears her love proudly in a patch on her jacket,

She refuses to be silent, instead puts up a racket,
She watches the Tonys with an awe she knows not of
And hears the words 'love is, love is, love is, love, is
love.'

She learns her love is holy,
She learns she is holy
And she'll never have to stay hidden.

Addendum:
You deserve to love whoever you want
And you deserve to put that love in whatever font.

Addendum:
No one is allowed to tell you who to be
And no one is allowed to tell you who to put into your
'we'.

Addendum:
You are every star in the sky,
Every young child reaching out to say hi,
Every world full of life and love,
Every mouth shouting prayers to above.

You are every smile that brightens a day,
Every spring morning in the month of May,
Every Phoenix rising from the flame,
So go ahead and win your acclaim.

Imagine:
The queer teen lives her life with the freedom of fire.

Addendum:
Her love lifts her higher, higher, higher.

29. Fairytale of Pink and Gold
Levi Lichy

Bio: I like watching wrestling and playing video games.

Email: Leviluther@icloud.com

*****

Want to hear a fairytale?
What fairytale do you want to hear today?
Cinderella?
Little Mermaid?
How about Rapunzel?
Oh I know, Sleeping Beauty!
Actually, wait, no… I've got a more riveting fairytale
today.

Locks of pink so fine and bright,
They make the Sun light up with joy,
Locks of blonde, locks of golden hair,
Nobody can dare grace the Queen's presence,
Not a hare,
Not a scared child,
Not even the wild.

Locks of pink, locks of gold
Though you may be a few years older than me,
I still wish to bring gifts to thee.

Locks of pink, locks of gold

Though you may know I must tell you so
That you, locks of pink and locks of gold,
You bring me a hypnotic spell that consumes me so,
Locks of pink, locks of gold
I must say it so that I wish to be your knight.
Whether a knight of the court or a jester of the court,
I wish to be within your castle walls,
O, locks of pink and locks of gold.

Though I've told this tale many times before,
Many have come, many have gone,
I wish to prove everyone wrong,
That you, my locks of pink and locks of gold,
That you are the one I never wish to wrong.

Locks of pink, locks of gold,
Why do you desire so to throw me away to the
guillotine?
Was I ever so mean to you?
Did I say a spell to curse your gold locks,
Or did you just never give a fuck about me?
Locks of pink locks of... no, no.
I was locked.
I was locked for a queen to turn treachery upon me.
I did not dare speak wrong,
I did nary dare speak ill,
I did never wish her killed.

I was locked,
I was locked,
All I did was give a fuck but now,

Locks of pink watch my head get chopped within a
blink.
Locks of a gold watch me turn
From a mold of a man to a blood-red old tale of an
idiotic soul.

Locks of gold,
Locks of pink,
I was locked,
I was locked,
You never gave a fuck.

30. I Love You
Sakura

Bio: I'm just your average teen poet, putting all my feelings into words and sharing them with the world.

Email: sakurajnalee@gmail.com

*****

some days when i wake up my first thought is "i love
you"
to whom it may refer,
i don't know
but to the stranger who visits me in my dreams,
sweeps me up and kisses me in the clouds,
twirls me around and around in the middle of meadows,
floats alongside me in the sea of serenity,
thank you,
thank you for the butterflies you have given me
and the mornings when i wake up so happy to be alive.
all i can say is, please come again,
i have many more "i love you"s
and many more clouds to soar through,
so come back to visit or maybe even stay
for you are the love of my dreams
and i shall forever be your queen.

31. Not My Fairytale
Sakura

Bio: I'm just your average teen poet, putting all my feelings into words and sharing them with the world.

Email: sakurajnalee@gmail.com

*****

every time i read a book i fall in love again,
not with the story,
but with you,
the boy who walks into the library just to make a ruckus,
catching my eye like a fish in a hook
and walks over just to ask what i'm reading
even though you already know,
through the smirks and chuckles and my sighs and rolled
eyes,
you cradled my heart like a newborn and kissed it
gently.
on the days you'd be with another,
my heart cried because knowing i wasn't your only one,
hurt
knowing that forever only lasts a month, hurts.
so whenever i read a book and glance over it to take a
peek,
i look for you,
for my knight in jester's attire,
the one who taught me that fairytale love stories
will only ever be a fairytale.

32. Cut
Erik Mercado

Bio: I love words, phrases and finding meaning behind simple things. Writing has always been a strong passion of mine. It's the safety of a blank page that makes me feel free and welcomed. I'm a college student at CSUF. Other hobbies include singing and making music.

*****

let's be actors, stars,
shine your light on me,
bring that passion that's meant for tv,
love me with that seamless movie star charm,
pretend it's written for me to be in your arms.
love me, together for the camera lens
before they yell 'cut' and it all ends.

33. Stolen
Maliyah Hicks

Bio: I'm a 15-year-old sophomore from San Diego, CA. I enjoy reading, writing, and music. I love sharing my thoughts and opinions as well as learning from others!

Instagram: maliyah.xo

*****

a black girl,
in a white world.
it's like a constant maze.
go left,
no, now right.
at this point,
i'm in a daze.
never correct,
always wrong.
but in your eyes,
it shouldn't phase me.
just "keep your head up"
or "change what you're doing"
and it'll all be okay.
but no.
i'm tired of you getting credit for all of my great ideas.
you take and you take from my fountain of wonders
and expect me not to be pissed.
but oh "i'll be fine," right?
all i have to do is make a small 'shift'.

no, that's all done with,
now i'm truly mad.
I need my respect,
and oh yeah, give back everything i had.
my ideas,
my style,
my speech,
my talents.
let it be used at my command
and i know it may be hard
to find your own originality
but taking mine,
that's not gonna work.
so with that, i must say,
please learn from these mistakes
because next time,
i'll be even more hurt.
i've got one last question,
something i've never felt.
how'd it feel,
to not have to work or fight for your respect?
to have everything in your life given?
is it nice?
calm?
or maybe even boring,
to never have to work for your own 1st place trophy?

34. Stand Up
Eliza

Bio: I am obsessed with writing poetry and would love to become a poet and have my own books.

Instagram: elizaarlene

*****

Stop the hate,
Stop the bullying,
Stop being mean,
Take a stand.

We, as the human race,
Have a job - no,
A responsibility
To stand up for others.

We all were given voices
Whether it be a voice to be heard or seen,
Let's use our voices to stand up for one another,
We have a responsibility.

It's "how can I respond using my abilities"
Not, "am I able to respond"
We all are capable of responding
To something.

Let's stand up for what is right,

You may be standing alone
And that is okay,
It takes one to change.

I say it again,
Stop the hate
Stop the bullying
Stop being mean
Take a stand.

We, as the human race,
Have a job - no,
A responsibility
To stand up for others.

To the bystanders
We, victims of bullying
Are asking you to help us:
You have been given voices
Please speak when we can't.

Please stand when
We are too weak,
Please step in
When you see us being bullied.

And to the victims
Of bullying
Un-velcro the insults.
They are words
That don't define who we are.

We are strong
We are fighters
We are going to be okay.
Most importantly,
We have an army of people
Willing to stand up for us.

35. K
Shivani Karne

Bio: I'm a graduate student in New York majoring in human resource management.

Instagram: shivani_karne_

*****

You would call it a squandered effort but it wasn't for me.
You would even be scorned of how we felt around each other, just glee.

I embrace you even in the dearth of your cologne,
I approbate you despite your mysterious tone.

I pushed some boundaries yet got stuck in a closed space.
A peaceful pasture is what I expected, all I got is a nebulous gaze.

Will I ever be gifted for unmasking our alliance?
Or will I forever in time expatiate this dalliance?

If ever we got a do over, I wouldn't change even for wit.
I'd rather mourn what we had than to never have it.

36. I Put On a Mask
Isabel Dorsey

Bio: I struggle with anxiety and BPD but writing has helped me to express what sometimes feels inexpressible.

Instagram: isabel_mariahhh

*****

I woke up one Friday morning, a morning of March
2020.
I turned on the news and you know what they said?
They said, "Put on a mask, you no longer get to choose."
So I put on a mask and I went to the store.
When I got back I did school, talked to friends, did
homework and more.
I put on a mask and I put on a smile
But two weeks of spring break was much too long a
while.
I put on a mask but I lost my grin
And the things that were bright started to dim.
I put on a mask and I went to get food
But not even boba could lighten my mood.
I put on a mask and I went to get school books
But I can't go anywhere without hyper analyzing my
looks.
I put on a mask to go buy clothes
But I look at the girl in the mirror and I feel the way she
loathes.
I put on a mask but this time it wasn't to leave the house

It was so they'd shut up about my grades and stop asking
why I ate like a mouse.
I put on a mask just to keep them all happy
Lord knows I can't explain why I feel so crappy.
I put on a mask and I hang out with my friends
But even then my mind wonders when this all ends.
I put on a mask and then lock my door
And when I take it off the tears start to pour.

37. Metamorphosis
Siddhanth Pachipala

Bio: I am a Houston-based poet delving into the intricacies of the human condition and what makes us tick. A coffee enthusiast and Oxford comma loyalist, I play with language at the intersection between my first-generation American identity and Indian heritage, channeling my lived experience into poetry. My motto: "Sometimes I write words. Sometimes they make sense."

Email: siddhupachipala@gmail.com

*****

A world of silence, choked by mere hushes,
The clamors of life buried in ashes.
Humanity, bound by stifling muzzle,
Drowned in quietude without a struggle.

The blazes of Hemera break anew,
Trampling reticence with her morning dew.
Earth, a sea of parasols, conjures song,
Its rhythms rendering a people strong.

Beats unite, universal languages,
Healing scars wrapped tight under bandages.
Building bridges to shatter boundaries,
Music hides the silence of memories.

Transformed by melody, ringing of hope,

Forgotten the day of when sounds eloped.

38. Four Seasons
Siddhanth Pachipala

Bio: I am a Houston-based poet delving into the intricacies of the human condition and what makes us tick. A coffee enthusiast and Oxford comma loyalist, I play with language at the intersection between my first-generation American identity and Indian heritage, channeling my lived experience into poetry. My motto: "Sometimes I write words. Sometimes they make sense."

Email: siddhupachipala@gmail.com

*****

The seasons of life,
Shifting and morphing,
A new beginning:

The wind bites to spite,
Its icy tendrils cutting
The shadows of bare trees.

A verdant bounty
Blesses the blossoming Earth,
A splendor of life.

Divine radiance
Blankets the world in fire,
Igniting the hearth.

Fluttering shadows
Strike a metamorphosis,
Painting hues of hope.

39. As the Morphine Drops
Kali G

Bio: I am currently a Student Success Coach with City Year at my alma mater, Chief Sealth. Working with my partner teacher who was also my 8th grade teacher, I continue to support students during virtual instruction. Art has been and will always be a part of the way in which I understand the world through poetry and fiction, in a chapbook and novel that will be published, eventually.

Email: thekalig@gmail.com

*****

Cold blood-stained memories of hospitalizations
won't let me forget the strain
of crippling pain that caused a ripple
to creep across the brittle windowpane
that was once used to view fading futures.
At times, I wish the surgeon of my life
had to stitch disintegrating sutures
into the wounds, made with a butter knife.
At least then, the scars would blend in
with something akin to skin. Dreams of clarion
horizons have turned into unwelcome
apparitions that promise to threaten.

How am I to sleep with one eye open,
eighteen screws in spine, and no intestine?

40. Expectations
Judah King

Bio: I love to cook and I love the color blue.

Email: Judahja.king@gmail.com

*****

Everyone reveres me with high regard.
They all clap me on my back
and commend my entrance to college.
They are proud of my goals and believe I will succeed.
A xerox of what could've been.
I'm not the first, but everyone believes
I'll be the first to succeed.
The first associate.
The first bachelor, the first master
and the first doctor.

People demand more of me.
I am to prove I am not like my predecessors
and the ones before me.
I am to prove that I will excel.
Everyone wants me to be better.
Everyone wants me show
that I am a cut above the rest.

Can't we all just peacefully coexist?
Would you love me any less if I was like them?
Would you grow in contempt and scorn?

The pressure is sometimes frightening.
Sometimes I feel that too much
responsibility has been put on me.
I fear I may let them down.

All I want is to be successful.
I want to be happy.
Tears seldom fall from mine cheeks,
even when it is all too much.
If it's not one thing it's the other.

Over the years, I've learned.
Studied. Observed. In more ways than one.
No one cares about what I want.
When I voice my wants, they are heard as
screeching demands instead of peaceful appeals.
Somebody always wants something from me.
Expectations.

41. Love is
Judah King

Bio: I love to cook and I love the color blue.

Email: Judahja.king@gmail.com

*****

Love is...
Love is always making an effort
Love is waking up and doing that thing even if you
didn't want to
Love is trying your best
Love is butterflies
Love lifts you off your feet
Love knocks you down
Love eviscerates
Love strengthens and weakens
Love is loquacious
Love is silent
Love is testing
Love is trying
Love is what makes a Subaru a Subaru
Love is what connects us
Love is
Never giving up.

42. Weathered Words
Edison Hicks

Bio: I am a young poet striving to make his mark on the world in whatever ways he can. I'm interested in both poetry and songwriting and have been writing for two years. My focuses in writing include the human condition, personal relationships, and the nature of art and creativity.

Email: edhicks91@gmail.com

*****

There is only one hurricane I remember,
A storm of ashes and skyward embers,
They fell on my head
But I felt instead
A frosted snow in December.

The sunlight shined on the yard,
So intensely that it could have charred
But the steam from the snow,
I saw that it refroze,
It left the earth scorched and scarred.

The windows shattered back into sand
As it fell through the cracks of my hand,
All my wounds were repaired,
All my demons were scared,
My trauma was a storm to withstand.

The weather's burden is immense
And rarely, it will ever make sense
But with you here with me,
With our old memories,
There no longer is any suspense.

As we're tied by a gold thread,
I now feel instead
Like I don't need to pretend.

43. Easier to Run
Edison Hicks

Bio: I am a young poet striving to make his mark on the world in whatever ways he can. I'm interested in both poetry and songwriting and have been writing for two years. My focuses in writing include the human condition, personal relationships, and the nature of art and creativity.

Email: edhicks91@gmail.com

*****

I've suffered cuts and bruises, all for the sake of us
And I'll suffer through them all again.
You will be protected from them.
I'll be the shield in front of my favorite soldier,
Saving him from his false fate.
When the world around us grows cold and bitter,
Let me cover you with my warmth and passion.
Let us hold onto each other in this city of phantoms.

I will dash to your arms so that I can give you safety.
I will burn in Hell for your eyes to look at me again.
I would drown in the rain to give you my breath,
To give you another chance at life.
I'll fight against life for this love to shine,
And I don't care if it's easier to run.

And I know you'd say the same.

44. The Devil Offered Me a Rose
Sierra Myers

Bio: I live in a small town. Ripon, California to be exact. My favorite color is purple. Reading, drawing and writing poetry are just a few of my hobbies.

Instagram: luna_ocean8

*****

The Devil offered me a rose today.
Admired by its blue beauty,
Intoxicated by its mournful smell,
I held the blue rose within my small hands
Like a fool.

I haven't noticed the thorns,
Impaling my cold skin
Like a fool
I didn't realize warm liquid was dripping down my forearm.
It was like the art of anesthesia captivated my body.

The Devil offered me a rose today.
Like a fool
I accepted it.

45. The Cycle of Your Script
Elizabeth Mata

Bio: I am something of an introvert, and I find that allowing the thoughts that cloud my madding mind to flow through my pen onto paper is much less difficult than speaking them into ears who may be hearing but not necessarily listening.

Instagram: you_smell_like_headache

*****

You are like a book, my love,
Which I compare you to often,
My favorite novel.
I read you,
You consume me.
All I do is sit in the sun and hold you,
Turning your pages,
I indulge in you.
I can never seem to take my eyes away,
For your plot is too beautiful.

But even then the story must end
As a book does,
And I will fall into a depression
When I reach the final page,
Read the last word,
This I know.

For you have become a part of me,
Your words a constant ring in my mind,
The story you tell has become mine,
I have fallen in love with your characters
And the perspectives you show me.

But, as nothing lasts forever,
You will end,
As will I,
And perhaps in another life
I will find you,
On a shelf
Collecting dust
And open your pages
And fall in love with you again.

46. Beauty and the Beast
Savannah Duffy

Bio: I'm a 27 year old writer and poet from Ohio.

Instagram: sa.savvy

*****

You told me you loved me
and I told you to take me home.
What you really felt was possession
and what I felt was oppression.
You wanted to put me up on a high shelf
where no one could reach me
and I just wanted to breathe.

But breathing wasn't an option with you.
It was either all or nothing
and I hated myself for who I made you.

I wish I knew then what I know now
and now I know you've always been this way,
you were just looking for a reason to let it out
of its cage and I gave it to you.
I became the cause of your hate,
the reason for your rage,
and all I ever wanted was to love you
because who better to love a monster than me?

47. Desiderium
Terrin Burton

Bio: I'm always in my head. Writing helps me get out.

Instagram: terrin.b

*****

Two birds,
One stone.
I'm the burden,
The rock thrown,
They were fragile
As the owl's home.
Vacant sign
Without the no,
Death's lone friend,
The crying moon,
The wolves join.
It's them I owe
Their siren song,
Lead me home.

Two ravens
I forgot,
Rapport to strangers
With memories, thought
I could save us both
But only tore the cloth.
Your candle held

Up to the moth,
Attraction only
Lasts so long.
Decathect
The feeling's gone,
Sunshine fades
And shadows grow.
Lose everything
As life goes on,
The seed you planted
Yet I still rot.

48. Terminal Velocity
Terrin Burton

Bio: I'm always in my head. Writing helps me get out.

Instagram: terrin.b

*****

Spiraling down
Merry-go-round
At a sickening speed,
We've been thrown away
And reaching out
In a sea of arms.
There are no hands to hold,
Now reaching
Terminal velocity,
These great men
Have sold our souls
That they may live forever.

Rise and take everything you please
For granted,
Remain unholy
And awaken what you fear most
From inside you.

All things in moderation
Jubilation has been stripped
From me, the clothes off my back

Have become me.

Ghostly, a mere reflection
Of what I once was,
Now a shell
To be taxidermied
And hidden away.

Manikins, animate and control.
Machines, divide and take hold.
Marauders, leave no man unstoned.
Merry-go-round, leave me alone.

49. I'm Leaving Tonight
Ky Liwag Lindsey

Bio: I'm a 14 year old with big dreams. Poetry for me is a way of escape, a road beyond reality when the steps for my big dreams trip me. Sometimes I write every night. Other times I don't write for months. That's just how it is.

Instagram: ky.the.space.goose

*****

maybe i'll leave,
go anywhere but here
to listen to russian music
and completely lose it.

go visit some old friends
who weren't with me 'til the end
like they said
they would be.

or even perhaps,
rob a grocery store
and later come back for more,
and leave without a trace.

maybe cry in the pouring rain
and scream in pain,
though i know i'm alright
maybe it's needed.

i don't know what i'll do
but i know that one day,
i'll yell, "i'm leaving tonight"
and they'd let me without a fight.

50. Pitter Patter
Ky Liwag Lindsey

Bio: I'm a 14 year old with big dreams. Poetry for me is a way of escape, a road beyond reality when the steps for my big dreams trip me. Sometimes I write every night. Other times I don't write for months. That's just how it is.

Instagram: ky.the.space.goose

*****

it's pouring outside
but it doesn't matter
because i love the sound
of the pitter patter.

and the cars passing,
on and on,
maybe they are looking for answers
and have been since dawn.

they drove and drove
because who really has a destination
at 3 am,
all they have is contemplation.

they're looking for themself
out in the pouring rain,
but who is going to tell them
that the only thing out there, is pain.

51. An Excerpt from Her Mind
Taraisa

Bio: I like reading and contemplating man's existence. (Yes, I know that's quite odd for a 17 year old haha!) I like to paint and I'm an avid music listener. My room always smells like incense and melting candles :)

Instagram: dezzyara

*****

She searched the planes of a shallow mind,
and poured over texts as old as time
to make sense of this world that spun on its axis,
and understand the motives of the masses.
She wanted to know what man had to gain
from causing his fellow such visceral pain.
But whether young or old they had no clue
as to what man did or why he would do.
But from such a young age she had to learn
that the fires we make can cause others to burn.
So whether it be big or small these truths she'd find,
they'd stay ingrained in the back of her mind
to teach her young pupils whose minds would hunger
for a lesson never taught when she was younger.

52. Paper Cranes
Journee Adams

Bio: When I was 15, my friend told me to never stop writing. I guess I try to listen.

Instagram: when_night_falls_

*****

I craft small paper cranes from Post-its,
Too small for me to crease and fold with my hands
So I rely on fingers tiptoeing across folded lines,
I align separate sides
So I don't get stuck with adhesive
But I'm stuck with an imperfect square
With jagged torn edges,
I look at them and say, "I feel you"
And move on.

There's no room for perfectionism in pocket origami,
No time for perfectly lined up sides,
Or triangles just right,
I fold out of personal obligation,
Allowing my mind to rest,
Settling into repetition,
Simply follow through on folds,
Nonsensically folding,
Halved horizontally,
Diagonally,
A blur of diamonds and triangles,

Memorized and uninstructed
Like they guide me themselves.

I used to make paper cranes,
Big and small and smaller,
I never knew how to break habits,
Small and big and bigger,
Making them my coping mechanisms,
Making them until I didn't need them anymore,
Left me with twitches in my fingers and all these birds
That didn't know how to fly away,
They let me get away from myself.
But migration season was over,
My frozen-over winter mentality was melting
Around these birds of spring,
They were left sans solstice,
Days too short to enjoy the light,
I left them in the dark,
Told them to stay where I'd find them,
Told them I'd be back
Because the need comes back.
A lack of control made into paper cranes
And released like doves at weddings,
Married to my obsession
But I took off the ring
And my cranes were lost to me,
No more of their dance,
Rhythm gone,
I was okay because I no longer needed
The repetition of beating wings.

My physical manifestation of coping

Of stress,
I never hoped that I'd end with flocks of birds crafted
from fingertips,
Making more
And making more,
Making them so that I can get over this mess.
These birds cloud my brain
And crowd my bags,
Becoming a weight carried with me
So I let them go.
Without holding on to tiny paper cranes,
My hands are open,
Relaxing into a pattern of stillness,
A habit of calm,
Fingertips no longer bent from meticulously creasing
paper wings
And a tiny paper crane at rest in my pocket,
In case I ever need it again.

53. Miss You
Journee Adams

Bio: When I was 15 my friend told me to never stop writing. I guess I try to listen.

Instagram: when_night_falls_

*****

i don't see the value in continuing to miss you,
i missed you long before you were gone,
i missed you before we met and my heart got strung along
and my past got in the way with my abandoned child mentality,
we slid past the formalities,
automatically exchanging a little piece of my heart for yours.

i had seen this all before,
clinging like the wrap that you cover your food with
and leave it too long,
and it expires,
this hesitance and patience breed rot,
i'm not just someone for playing with,
you aren't supposed to play with your food.

this love was consuming
and i,

i have been making up for lost time since before the
beginning
because my beginnings left me feeling,
a little less loved and a little less grounded
and i lost myself,
buried in your arms,
dazed by the words off your lips,
i miss the times when we would talk about nothing.

i miss pretending to listen
but it didn't come as easily for me as it did for you,
i easily let things get tangled in my memories
and i only use bluetooth headphones
because undoing knots made my fingers crick and
cramp,
and ain't nobody got time to be wrapped up
in those kind of messes.

it's kinda hard to forget
when we see the garden for the flowers
and not the weeds.
in my down time,
i've been
slowly digging up all the things i don't need
and maybe take the time to make my flowers
a safe place from you
and maybe they'll teach me
how to grow.

and let go.

let me learn that missing you is a weakness

and it's okay to be weak
because the rain may give us strength to bloom again.

54. Who Needs Forever
Alexandria Milne

Bio: I prefer the pronouns she/her, I am 17 years old and just beginning to figure out who I am.

Instagram: allie.n.milne

*****

Stay for a while,
Let us look at the stars, together.
If not forever, just a tad bit longer,
One more glance at those eyes before you disappear
Because that's what you always do.
At least stay tonight
And we'll act as if the stars are the only thing in sight.

55. Broken Because of You
Alexandria Milne

Bio: I prefer the pronouns she/her, I am 17 years old and just beginning to figure out who I am.

Instagram: allie.n.milne

*****

I needed you to go
But I wanted you to stay,
My broken heart would be filled if only you'd stay away
Yet, here I am letting you in
Because I feel alive inside and at that moment
A few broken pieces seemed fine.

56. Anaphora
Benjamin Johnson

Bio: I love Tennis.

Instagram: lilgangstablueberry

*****

I hear a line of a song and fear
I'll find it wrong when I fall in love,
I hear a hatred growing instilled in me
In sighs and hums when I fall in hostility.
I hear the TV and steps and shattered chains
Hitting the floor when I fall with a hard rain,
I hear a line of a song and repeat it slowly
So my love can breathe it in,
I hear a hatred slowing
And when it starts again I'll fend it off.
I hear the TV and it's me in a scene I wrote
And I hope it's a change that lasts.
Hope is a change at last.

57. We America
Kya Baker

Bio: I'm 16 years old and I love the arts - dance, theatre, singing, writing, you name it.

Email: kyabaker04@gmail.com

*****

Like a turbulent tornado it hit so quick,
Yanking victims from homes to hospital beds,
Seeking an unfathomable destruction,
Something we cannot ponder in our own little heads.

The rage began for months on end, no sign of winding up,
The news coverage wasn't news
Without showing the death toll rising up,
Rising dip-less and drop-less as it ran amok.

The stench of death reeked in the towns,
In the cities and counties it knew no bounds as it
Spread like the fires that came in last year,
No intent of calming down.

It is fierce - yet we are fiercer,
We have overcome challenges far greater,
In order to fight it we go without rest,
Trying to seek wisdom that we already possess.

We are stronger than we give ourselves credit for,
Our light and our power, let us not tremble nor,
Give in to the darkness as it travels town to town,
City to city and bound to bound.

For as we all know light cannot break,
Scientifically that ability is fake,
And if us the light are to progress through this trial,
We must not let it consume us while
We fight and fight and fight.

"United We Stand," he put it in ink,
Now more than ever let us not think
That our unity will ever waiver,
For we are stronger together!

58. Time Will Tell
Rebekah

Bio: I think freely under open skies, with the passing of miles, and while putting pen to paper. I'm an enthusiast of life and making moments matter for myself and for others. I write for self-expression and I write to be a voice for others. The pen speaks to me as much as I speak to it.

Instagram: rebekah.a97

*****

What would you call time if you knew its fleeting nature?
What would you call the passing of its grandeur?
If you stood in wealth would time fly or stand?
If you stood in squalid conditions would it never end?

In motionless turning our lives revolve
A diverse monotony we stubbornly carry on
By hours, minutes, seconds solved
Where always the end has only just begun.

Measured and spoonfed in doses of days,
We add sensory value to our outer space.
Forced ever onward with zero delays,
Stumbling and crumbling by our own brutal pace.

The machine ever ticking exacts its measurement
Broken into nth fractions of quantum size

We're scrambling and scratching to capture the moments
Slipping future, to present, to past... there it dies.

Circumstantial, spacial and respective of none,
Time is the enemy of those who seek it
And the friend of those who wish it done
It never relents, never cuts loose, never quits.

Time can tie your hands and free your soul,
The ultimate master when given full reign,
An obstacle or a scholarship on the road to your goal,
The cause or the doctor for all of your pain.

What an angelic gift, what indispensable treasure,
Bequeathed at birth disposed of at death,
Hold fast by it, don't squander at leisure,
Once taken by whim it will drain all your strength.

Time is the ultimate powerful illusion,
A transient monster that is empty inside,
It promises ever a cosmic resolution
But simply created by God to stable our minds.

Be its friend, take its hand but don't let it fool you
Time is your allotment, do not let it down.
It's passing, it's fleeting, it's hardly even true
But without it right now, in eternity you'd be found.

And the question only remains... which eternity?
Only time will tell.

59. Clutter of the Mind
Barrett Ahn

Bio: I am an aspiring author and high school student in Los Angeles. My work has been recognized by the National Scholastic Art and Writing Awards, Teen Ink, The Decameron Project, and more. I hope to continue to mature as a writer.

Email: barrett.endell@outlook.com

*****

I see black and white and grey,
I see too many colors of different shades,
A whole world in here,
I should get away from here.

Filled to the brim.

I know darkness
In my mind,
Like the night sky,
Like the basement you were scared of as a child.
I know light
In the places I can find,
Confinement and freedom,
Reflection and reason.

Filled to the brim.

Hoarding thoughts in my head,
Boxes and boxes of them,
Clutter is a feeling,
Sifting through it for hours,
I don't know where to start,
Too much swimming around in my mind
If I break they will flow out in a stream.
Quietly overwhelmed,
Silently drowned,
Every now and then
Constant influx of realization,
Perceptions and observations,
Ideas, feelings, dreams,
Sadness, tears - tearing at the seams
Of my mind's layers.
Dickinson was right,
"The brain is wider than the sky,"
Though sometimes it feels
As shallow as my sigh.

60. Bewitching Venom
Natalie E McKenty

Bio: I am a Chicago based daydreamer that finds sanity in writing, photography, and illustration. I like to call myself a creator instead of a writer, artist, or photographer, because for me words are like paint or a camera. They are all simple tools one can use for the purpose of expression.

Instagram: m_natalie_art1

*****

2 am,
You've come to take me again.

Your heel prints upon my mattress,
My peace turns to your madness,
I become as wee as the little hare of Alice.

Creeping in the shadows of my blind spot,
There is always the same nagging thought,
Spreading faster than black rot,
It bites into my flesh leaving the blood to clot.

For I am but a prisoner of bone and cells,
Always falling victim to the alluring ways of your spells.

They blur and bleed into each tranquil dream,
Poisoning my self-made heaven
With your

Bewitching venom.

3 am
You've made my room your den.

Tugging me down off my pillow,
My nausea creeps and comes with a bellow,
The blankets torn away like thin phyllo.

Never going away till you're done,
My terror is your readymade fun,
For your only enemy is the punctual sun
However. before then I can only wish to run

For I am but a kite in ballet slippers spinning about,
Always helplessly gliding through the ceiling air
With the same peculiar route.

It's a violating feeling that seeps through my sickened
flesh,
Leaving me weary at your never-ending vendetta
With your
Bewitching venom.

4am
You're an enemy more inescapable than wicked men.

I now fear what is supposed to be a peaceful escape,
Never will I know your exact shape,
My sanity you pluck off me like a grape.

I try to say no before you start,

You are of no heart,
There is no beauty in your art,
In my life, you are sadly a part.

For I am but your unwilling person,
Always you are trying to lengthen our song,
By putting another verse in.

It is what haunts me even when you're not here,
You will always be a soulless being that will never be
welcomed
With your
Bewitching venom.

61. Bluebird
Natalie E McKenty

Bio: I am a Chicago based daydreamer that finds sanity in writing, photography, and illustration. I like to call myself a creator instead of a writer, artist, or photographer, because for me words are like paint or a camera. They are all simple tools one can use for the purpose of expression.

Instagram: m_natalie_art1

*****

Bluebird, thou never do sing,
Yes, to the world thou just bow as if it's thy king.

I do forget what it sounded like,
Was it reminiscent of the whistling of the piper's pipe?

Because thou art just a Bluebird
That cherishes someone else's dried roses.

Bluebird, have thou ever dreamt of a ring?
Yes, thou ponder on how it would make up for the flaws in thy left wing.

I do not think such a gem suits thee
Thou would believe it to be a charitable borrow and not a true devotee.

Because thou art just a Bluebird

That cherishes someone else's dried roses.

Bluebird, will thou come back in the spring?
Yes, but the still present cold to thy glass bones will
cling.

I do though still remember thy smile,
It's under the scrutiny of others cracks like old tiles.

Because thou art just a Bluebird
That cherishes someone else's dried roses.

Bluebird, thou stopped perching on thy favorite swing,
Yes, now thou just makes a nest out on a thrown away
rusty old thing.

I do recall how thou wishes for everyone else's dreams,
Was their pettiness worth all thy torn seams?

Because thou art just a Bluebird
That cherishes someone else's dried roses.

Bluebird, for thou the raindrops will always sting,
Yes, they like every missed chance pierce through thy
drums with a ping.

I do know thy eulogy will haunt as it speaks,
It will tell of a romantic frail creature with tear stained
cheeks.

Because thou art just a Bluebird
That cherishes someone else's dried roses.

62. Me
Katie

Bio: I love music and writing and if I could do those two
things for the rest of my life, I'd be happy.

*****

getting back on my feet was tough i'll admit,
but i knew that i would get through this
it's been so long since that day,
and i keep getting stronger along the way
singing the same song over and over
helped me get through that tough time,
i never realized how strong it made me
to admit that i wasn't fine
my friends never left my side,
even though i tried to hide
finding light when there was only darkness,
i'm still not who i once was
but someday i know i'll be me.

63. Record Player
Tori Baker

Bio: I first started taking writing seriously freshman year, when I joined our school's Writing Club. I had always been writing, but had never considered it as a potential career path. Now this is what I'm going to school for, in hopes of being an English teacher, and publishing works throughout the year, spending my summers writing. This is what I love!

Instagram: my.baby.moon

*****

I used to dance to my record player,
Sometimes he'd dance with me too.
Though we were together for hours,
It always ended too soon.

I used to dance to my record player,
He says it's like I'm in color again.
But I know it's not the meds,
It's the music that's keeping me from Them.

I used to dance to my record player,
I wish we could've stayed that way,
Holding me tightly in his arms
As if I might float away.

I used to dance to my record player

And as I jumped and swayed,
I realized I was better again
So I put all my pills away.

I used to dance to my record player
Until I was taken from my home,
Put in a white, bland room
With people I don't know.

I used to dance to my record player,
They say I cut off my ear
Because the Voices were so loud
And the music was too quiet to hear.

I used to dance to my record player,
He can't visit me today.
The doctors tell me I'm dangerous
But the doctors don't know what They say.

I used to dance to my record player
But now I'm stuck here,
So for now I'll have to settle
For the ringing in my ear.

64. Dealer's Choice
Yenny Coll

Bio: I am a writer, dreamer, lover, teacher, and much more. You can read more of my poetry on my Instagram or check out my other writings on my website, www.yennycoll.info

Instagram: yennycollcomfort

*****

Down a winding road,
I strolled, totally whole,
until I came across a fork
and my heart froze.

Both paths to me called,
one familiar but raw,
the other uncertain though I was enthralled
and I swing both ways like a seesaw.

Unable to split my soul in two,
afraid of what I'd lose if I choose,
I stand in place, unable to move.
It's a choice I'd rather altogether remove.

Inaction is an act of deciding, and
in between all this internal fighting
I'm trapped in a whirlpool of abiding
by the unnatural demands that are overriding

the power within. Watch it coincide
with the abdication of lies
To oneself retreating to the ease
Of past selves.

65. Memories We Create
Yenny Coll

Bio: I am a writer, dreamer, lover, teacher, and much more. You can read more of my poetry on my Instagram or check out my other writings on my website, www.yennycoll.info

Instagram: yennycollcomfort

*****

I see you in the trees
As their green swish-and-sways.
I smell you in the rain
As it pitter-patters on the window pane.
I feel you in the breeze
That ruffles my hair
And in between the grains
Of sand that remain so unaware.
I hear you in the canned beer sizzle pops
I taste you in the crunch of taco food truck stops
As they steer clear of here.
I sense you in the rumble of rubber on gravel
And in the memories of pain that grapple
With my mind.

But I take it in my stride as you decide
What to show and what to hide
In the hide of your skeletons
That sleep in your closet.

So let's unlock it, and
Crop it so it fits neatly
In the picture frame locket
That I keep on my window pane
As I watch the rain
And the trees and the breeze and the sand
Take one last beautiful stand
And pose for the memory
That I chose to create
Out of crushed beer cans
And greasy taco plates.

66. Something Else
Carolyn

Bio: I know just that I am

Instagram: rebel_red23

*****

It doesn't hurt
the way it would ripping off a bandaid.
Nor does it viscerally ache,
burrowed buried beneath your skin.

It's something else.

A fear that memory is deja vu;
that I will have to find you, all over again
somewhere else, someone else
and you won't know me.

So I'll keep your eyes in my life
'til our paths are so far passed
I can't see you anymore.

And something else becomes us.

67. Autumn's Curse
Rogue Clawson

Bio: I began writing poetry to help cope with my depression. It provided the means for me to express my feelings in a way that was both healthy and productive. I always found it to be quite beautiful, like a shard of your soul laid out on paper. I've since overcome my depression, but I still use poetry as a means of channeling my pain into something that gives back to the world.

Instagram: rogueclawson

*****

Cold air, colder eyes
All you've ever known is lies
And as your heart sinks in fear,
You know deep down that autumn's here.

Death knocks at your door,
You know you've heard that sound before,
Your heart fills with dread,
Everyone you know is dead.

He says it's called the Autumn's Curse,
The rules are really quite perverse,
The graves sing out for a friend,
You never got to make amends.

You plead for winter to come sooner,

Maybe next year he'll take fewer
But once you bid the fall adieu,
You'll realize there's nobody left but you.

68. The EscApe
Eric D. Cherny

Bio: I listen to Metal and play Dungeons & Dragons.

Instagram: eric_the_cherny

*****

Screaming with my fists in the air so you can hear me,
Nothing will change and I don't even care says the
insurgency,
I have to go home or you'll kick me out but that's a
fallacy,
I have to climb and I have to shout so they remember
me,
The tallest branch won't reach the top,
The mountain climbs where the river stops.

Bananas fuel the power cruel, live your life, embrace the
doom.

Behold the baboon, aggression entombed,
Relax and elate as you masturbate!

We sit at cut logs getting straight A's
But wait anyway because you're not a man today.

How do I know what to keep as my own?
I ask the Divine to leave me alone,

You can't atone for what you can't control,
The truth is kept in restricted zones,
And you can't trust your chromosomes!

69. The Wind
Carlos A. Lemos

Bio: I'm a young writer, musician, music producer, video editor, and YouTuber. I'm based out of the state of New Jersey and starting writing poetry in 2017. Ever since, I've been writing poetry and now I'm starting to write a novel. After highschool I want to pursue a career in education, specifically in history and possibly in English.

Instagram: d.o.c.c_music

*****

As the tempest grows and winter sings its woes,
The winds of its cry wisp and whirl in the atmosphere
Causing the trees to swing to and fro,
Clearing the leaves left behind from fall,
For the wind leaves no leaf,
For with each day the wind extends leaving no frontier.

As the tempest grows with the temperature dipping low,
Those who can take refuge in their homes do so.
However the wind works around the clock with no stop
Until the Lord himself deems their work sufficient,
For the wind travels in all seasons,
Even when no seed can become a crop.
Even so, the wind in spring helps the reproduction of crops,
That it can be more efficient.

The wind now lays low after it's work is finished.
The people complain, saying, "Where art thou, oh wisp of wind?"
They wonder why the wind has settled down,
Many thinking it's the wind's penance,
That it regrets its good work for man,
When in reality, the wind has already followed the will of the Lord.
It's purpose is founded on nature, neither being good nor horrendous.

As we reach the end, the inevitable hour,
The Lord will use the natural things to finish His work.
The wind is like the prophets of old:
When the Lord speaks it is obedient, and answers not in sourness,
When the Lord orders, the wind is as fast
As a legion of Ottoman janissaries,
Never before seen, winning almost every battle, so help them God.

The wind, I wish God's speed to the wind,
For it, like many legends, is like a force of energy,
A force that binds us all; may it lead us toward a memory,
A distant time before sin was rampant, and it cursed our kin.
May the wind make miracles,
Like the time when God had split the red sea with wind.
Then when it's all settled, may it be like when Christ calmed the sea.

The wind obeyed the Lord's command, so why should
we fear?

70. A Thank You Letter
Makenzie N Strickler

Bio: I love reading, writing and theatre. All these are things I know I can turn to to express myself and to relax from the rest of the world. I'm a junior starting the International Baccalaureate program in the fall.

Email: oceanfeather09@gmail.com

*****

What do you say,
when you've had the time of your life?
What do you say,
when that time is over?
Would words even suffice?
When all the time spent laughing, and sharing, and loving,
is finally over?

What can I say,
Now that it's really over?
What should I say,
for all you've given me,
for all you've done for me,
for all the smiles, the encouragement?
Oh, the encouragement!
The words I'll treasure and carry with me all my life.
And the time?
The time you gave to me.

To us.
To this.

Then, I guess,
I'll say all there is to say,
Thank you.

71. Trending to be Miserable
Ayesha

Bio: I am 17 and I am a mental health advocate.

Instagram: denteddpearll

*****

We're spreading hate,
We're losing faith,
"Fuck others feelings, they didn't care about mine."
So you're spreading that bitterness
That was given to you once upon a time?
Two wrongs don't make it right.

Let's stop coddling and give people the truth,
Instead of giving them useless advice,
We're contacting our toxic exes
That gives us the attention we can't give ourselves.
These accounts that text your boyfriends or girlfriends
To check if they are cheating,
Benefit off your insecurities.
We post about hating ourselves,
We're having sex just to forget,
We're questioning our own life
But manifesting it in relationships.

We're bored so we're starting drama,
We're getting high to forget the lows in life,
We're drinking to forget thinking,

We overshare every detail of our lives,
We're not giving ourselves time to grow,
We want to stay in this moment of woe,
We're followers instead of leaders,
Dominoes fall, so do cheaters.
We're people pleasers for people who don't even see us
as people,
The light shown from the blinds is too light for our dark
minds,
We're in this tunnel and trying to find a way to get out.

You can shout,
You can scream
And that's fine.
Let out those emotions that can harm you in the long
run,
Don't give up and be done,
You can dream,
You can learn to be okay alone,
To love the body you're in and that's shown in the
mirror.
You wish to not look at,
You can get the help you need,
You can feed the kid who was robbed of their childhood
By not loving themselves at a young age.
You can end a chapter and turn the page,
You can go at your own pace,
You can feed the kid who was robbed of their childhood
in general.

Everyone has a different story,
I don't know you and you don't know me.

Instead of running from your problems,
You can face what's staring you down at night,
You can fight the thoughts telling you to give up.
When a tear falls from your eyes,
You're gonna have times when you tell yourself it's not
worth it,
It's okay to have those days.

Let the good days have a mark like the bad days,
Post your talent, don't be afraid of what others are gonna
say,
Don't live in fear
Because people will say what they want anyway.
Instead of finding different ways to sabotage your
growth,
Learn about yourself,
Learn about others
Or both.
Learn your worth
Because we all know on this earth,
There is grass,
There are trees,
The breeze blows the leaves.
Beautiful things exist and are vibrant to the human eye,
Don't let the negativity in the world
Deceive you from your beautiful soul that's on the rise,
There is a lot of things we can universally say,
The number one thing is
WE NEED CHANGE.

I know we're still young and growing everyday,
No matter if we're 12 or 25,

We either change or we're going to see more people die,
Physically and inside.

72. I Fell in Like
Ayesha

Bio: I am 17 and I am a mental health advocate.

Instagram: denteddpearll

*****

It's almost that time again, when we first met
Fell in like at first sight, I wasn't ready for that yet.
My friends would ask me, "Why do you like him so much?"
I had no response because I didn't know myself,
More than a year and there are still tears on my pillowcase,
More than a year and I still see his face,
Even though there's not but my brain tells me there is.

Because that's what I wish,
To see him,
That one day we move on
From what me and him went through and start anew,
We apologize for the trauma,
We apologize for the drama,
I wouldn't have had to go through my last relationship
If we had just communicated.

Imagine if we didn't care about what our friends said
At the expense of our dime,
If we didn't seek that validation at the time,

If we didn't invite others into our problems
And just focus on how we feel on the inside.
It's hard to do so when we both have so much pride,
I want to talk to him but I don't want to get rejected,
I'm scared if I talk to him, we'll still be connected,
I can't handle these feelings by myself.

They say if you really love someone let them go
When I first heard that I didn't understand,
But now I know,
Even though I let him go
Because I wanted him to be with someone else
Yet wanted him all to myself
But I knew I was going down
And I didn't want you going down with me.
I was trying to do a selfless act,
That wasn't the way to do that.

I would do things just to get to him,
Acting like I wasn't, but who was I trying to kid?
Just caring about myself and not how it would affect
him,
Even though he would never admit it did,
I thought I could have what we had with other guys.
Didn't work, I tried.
I hated myself,
I hated him
Until I figured out what I had wasn't hate.
It was pain and anger because of what happened,
It was a constant heartache.

When I wasn't talking to him I felt I was over the
situation,
When I started talking to him all the feelings came back,
And it became complicated.
When he would say things to retaliate because of what
happened,
I would be mad when I didn't get my way,
Led to me texting things I didn't mean to say,
I affected someone I cared about in that way.

I'm giving him the space he wanted that I never
respected,
I'm leaving alone the scar, I don't even know if it's still
infected,
I'm falling apart knowing
That I don't know how he's doing.
I'm doing it for him,
I'm willing to go through all this
Like he did for me.
If he's happy,
If his heart is beating with fullness once again
Like I know it was when I met him.

I know he has probably changed,
I most likely don't know who he is anymore,
No matter what happens, he is someone I will always
care for.
Maybe this is the price to pay and it's a lot with which to
deal,
I guess that's what happens
If you fall in like before you are healed.

73. Tell Me More, Honey
Kimiko White

Bio: I have been writing poetry for as long as I remember. I've always used poetry as an outlet and lately, I've been experimenting with all kinds of different sounds.

Instagram: kiimikowhite

*****

your mouth drips with honey
i never noticed -
the way my honey's been sitting in the cabinet.
i eat these words like Winnie the Pooh
and because i can't get enough,
everyone knows where i've been.

the sweetest thing i've ever known
was like the kiss on a collar bone -
the aftertaste resides on the back of my tongue
my thoughts of you are essential
and you're always on the frontline
so everyone knows where i've been.

every so often, i leave pieces of you on sidewalks
and streetlights.
it sticks to my coats in the winter
leaves honey glazed tire marks on roads to get to you.
so wherever i go -
everyone knows where i've been.

74. Taste of the South
Kimiko White

Bio: I have been writing poetry for as long as I remember. I've always used poetry as an outlet and lately, I've been experimenting with all kinds of different sounds.

Instagram: kiimikowhite

*****

i like my yams with a side of baked mac and cheese,
brown-sugar sweet
and a cheesy spoonful with the crispy edges.
the only thing stronger than this fork,
is the two paper plates that's keeping it all together.
granny's praying to bless this food
and the hands that prepared it -
let's grab hands so i don't get tempted
to take a bite
of the south
and wrap it up in aluminum foil
so i'll have a plateful
when I go back home.

75. Stretch Marks
Kate M. Colome

Bio: I am a teenage Latina writer who enjoys displaying an adolescent perspective: self image, romantic/platonic love, and the juvenile mindset. Aspects of youth that fascinate me are what many experience but don't speak about. I like hearing the unmentionable and I cherish vulnerability. I write with the intention that others my age can find familiarity and comfort that their thoughts are normal.

Instagram: katem.colome

*****

When I first saw you, I couldn't believe my eyes.
You were what I wanted for so long; a blessing, a
miracle, a sign.
I was in denial that I would be oh so lucky to see you in
my life.
Since I had never seen you, I went to another woman for
answers -
my mother.
She told me what I wanted to hear and that I was right
about you.
I was victorious after years seeing the scale's numbers
increase;
granted, I lacked the physical manifestations.
Me and my body were hopeless.
A milestone in a journey to fill the mold

of what my body is supposed to look like.

Then my mom told me to get rid of you.

And other women besides her despise you as well.

They say you're ugly and unattractive,

or that you're what makes me and all young girls so.

So I grew ashamed of you and chose to hide you from the public eye.

But the thing is,

you're not embarrassing.

I find you naturally gorgeous and real.

Once I embraced you with awe again, I found that many agreed.

You're a symbol to and for me of growth.

Thanks for being there to remind me how far I've come.

76. Some Seuss is Loose
Thomas R. Cilluffo

Bio: I am an operatic tenor, craftsman, and casual writer. I have sung with various opera companies throughout the United States including Portland Opera, Opera Colorado, and the Santa Fe Opera. As a craftsman, I make bespoke conducting batons for choir and orchestra conductors all over the world. I enjoy writing about science and encouraging critical thought.

Email: tcilluff@gmail.com

*****

We are not banning all the tomes.
They are not banished from your homes.

Their information they beget,
is what the author should regret.

His publisher has made a choice,
to not print his racist voice.

It does not mean that Seuss is done.
Don't clutch your pearls, don't grab a gun.

The books you like are still out there.
But racist views, you should not share.

The racist books are out of date.

They always were. This was their fate.

They've not been pulled from shelves above.
They're not e'en books that you've heard of.

Not cat, nor hat, nor ham and eggs,
These books, now gone, are naught but dregs.

He's not been 'cancelled.' That's not correct.
If you're complaining, you're on, das Recht.

77. Mirror
Claire Boeck

Bio: I am a trans woman currently in college for a degree in Journalism. I love reading, and writing is a huge hobby of mine. I also have an interest in film and media production.

Instagram: claire.vs.the.world

*****

Sometimes I see her in passing,
In the corner of my eye,
In the reflection of a puddle.
She peeks at me and then scurries away.
She looks happy.

I stare into the mirror and she can't run.
She looks scared,
I look scared.
I place my hand against hers and we stare.
To her, I am but a memory
Of a block of marble from which
She sculpted, and was sculpted.
I am the block as well as the artist
Who chips away at the marble.

To her, I am but a memory.
To me, she is but a dream.

Frightening is the dream that threatens to be real.

78. Fire and Rain
Marlys Kutach

Bio: I'm a 17-year old high school student from the bay area. I've gotten into writing poetry and other forms of creative writing only recently during the pandemic, and it's something that's helped me through complicated and difficult times.

Instagram: maelys_writes

*****

You were like a fire to me,
You always were, that, I knew.
Ignited, entranced, and danced
Inside of me, this side of you,
I danced around that metaphor,
I plucked out the bits and parts
And threw the rest into the dark.

Blinded by the shining light,
Couldn't see in the obscurity,
You glowed with false integrity,
So articulate and meticulous
To manipulate and sell to us
A bouquet for our cries, they were empty promises,
An array of lies disguised as simply solace and
I was but a daisy in a field.

Small, unnoticed, my weakness revealed

Every petal and leaf totally unconcealed,
Without defense, without a shield,
So quickly swayed, so quickly won,
I would've stayed, I couldn't run.

Your lies were sweet as golden molasses,
Stuck in the trance of your beholden advances,
I smelled the smoke but not the direction,
I sensed the cracks but made no objection,
You told me, in my gaze was a reflection,
Created the flaws in my perception,
Invented the laws of what you call love
And I think you saw the storm gathering above.

I leaned in, got too close, and it burned,
Didn't feel it so I soon returned,
One can only take so much pain
Before the sadness turns to rage
And down falls the acid rain.

I smell your mark like burning sage,
Fire was born out of the desire to control,
The lure of the power, disregard for its toll,
Cradled and nurtured for far too long,
To put you out, I fear I'm not that strong,
I scamper away like a rabbit from the flames,
The unsettling feeling that things will never be the same.
"I've never felt so small," I said.
I live with a never ending sense of dread.

I think of you and I just see red.

Writer's Pocket

Writer's Pocket is a publication house that first started out as an Instagram page on February 15th, 2016 by 2 college students. We began with the aim of providing a platform for amateur writers and budding poets.

As a publication house, we publish new anthologies of short stories, poems and other forms of writing every month. Every piece of content in our anthologies is submitted by young writers from all over India. We are completely unbiased in the selection process and try to provide the best content to our readers.

We have also published several novels and stand-alone collections of short writings by single authors. If you want to check out any of the books published by us, you can visit www.writerspocket.com or search for us on Amazon!

Also published by Writer's Pocket

Novels

In Search Of Home *by VK Mehta and Mahek Sharma*
Autumn - The Mosaic Of All *by Roobal Gupta*
Tangled Up In You *by Tanaya Atre*
In Search Of Spring *by Shreya Shively*
The Third Eye *by Nikhil Yadav*

Stand-alone books by single authors

Neither Prose Nor Poetry *by Anuradha Bhide Phatak*
DuskyVibes *by Nikita Shah*
Chalice of Love *by Rohit K Kumar*
Naked Ordinance *by Mriga Bhasin*
Papercuts Leave Scars *by Nidhi Shah*
The God Within *by Ratika Mishra*
The Flower Princess *by Sehrish Shadab*
Fiction With A Tinge Of Reality *by Shivangi Mandhiyan*
Highly Unstable *by Mayank*
Impressions *by Dr. Nidhi Kakkar*
Meraki *by Jayamadure S.*
Nazar *by Anierroodh Raammie (Hindi)*
Seeding Thoughts *by Shivangi Thaker*
Hallucinations *by Herat Udavat (Gujarati)*
I Know I Don't Know *by Sonali Sharma*
A Wallflower *by Arjun Deshmukh*
Dusk Dreams *by Kaavya S*
From The Sunflower's Heart *by Vanalika Vaid*
Saudade - The Presence In Absence *by Rashmi Nirvikar*
The Spring Cologne *by Yashaswini Angiras*
Dhi's Oracle of Divine Epiphanies *by Saudamini Mishra*
Fitoor *by Qabeera (Hindi)*
You Are Poetry *by S.V. Aurelia*
Silent Din *by Mohammed Sami Khan*
Brokenmoon *by maré vad raven*
Ignited Inspiration *by Anjali Patel*
Her: Chronicles of an un-warrior *by Monika Bhargava*

Anthologies

Petrichor Of Words *(a collection of poems)*
Dream Catcher *(a collection of poems)*
Unsaid Truth *(a collection of poems)*
Elysian *(a collection of poems)*
Arsenic *(a collection of poems)*
Waiting For Sunshine *(a collection of poems)*
Field of Hues *(a collection of poems)*
Good Vibes *(a collection of poems)*
Extra Confetti *(a collection of stories)*
Midnight Dilemma *(a collection of poems)*
Summer Within The Pages *(a collection of poems)*
A Bouquet Of Words *(a collection of poems)*
Pillow Talks *(a collection of poems)*
Inked By Emotions *(a collection of poems)*
Apeiro *(a collection of poems)*
A Cluster Of Ballads *(a collection of poems)*
Rainbows In Black *(a collection of poems)*
Soul Candy *(a collection of poems)*
Sunflowers On The Horizon *(a collection of poems)*
Spilled Emotions *(a collection of poems)*
And A Poet Was Born *(a collection of poems)*
To Brighter Days *(a collection of stories)*
Always & Forever *(a collection of letters)*
Through The Eyes Of Dragonflies *(a collection of poems)*
Kalamna Mukhe *(a collection of Gujarati stories)*
Poet's Paradise *(a collection of poems)*
Writer's Unboxed: Uncensored *(a collection of stories)*

You can check out these books at
www.writerspocket.com and Amazon.in!

Made in the USA
Las Vegas, NV
30 August 2021

29280656R00097